D1162354

Nature's Children

TICKS

James Martin

GROLIER

FACTS IN BRIEF

Classification of Ticks

Subphylum: *Chelicerata* (chelicerates)

Class: *Arachnida* (arachnids—group including spiders and scorpions)

Order: *Acari* (ticks and mites)

Species: At least 860 species of ticks. There are at least 45,000 species of mites.

World distribution. Ticks limited to areas where their hosts live; mites live all around the world, in all habitats.

Habitat. Soft ticks mainly live in nests and burrows of hosts; hard ticks in forests and grasslands. Their close relatives, mites, occur practically everywhere.

Distinctive physical characteristics. Young ticks have six legs, but later molt to gain an extra pair; body has just one section; most mites are extremely small.

Habits. All ticks visit hosts to feed on blood.

Diet. Ticks feed only on blood of mammals, birds, and reptiles.

© 2004 The Brown Reference Group plc
Printed and bound in U.S.A.
Edited by John Farndon and Angela Koo

Published by:

GROLIER

An imprint of Scholastic Library Publishing
Old Sherman Turnpike, Danbury, Connecticut 06816

Library of Congress Cataloging-in-Publication Data
Martin, James W. R.
  Ticks / James W. R. Martin.
    p. cm. — (Nature's children)
  Includes index.
  Summary: Describes the physical characteristics, habits, and natural environment of ticks.
  ISBN 0–7172–5957–9 (set)   ISBN 0–7172–5975–7
  1. Ticks—Juvenile literature. [1. Ticks.] I. Title. II. Series.

QL458.M37 2004
595.4'29—dc22

2003049180

Contents

Did you know that your body may be invaded by tiny eight-legged animals that drink your blood? These animals are called ticks. Ticks drink the blood of other animals, too, including dogs, cats, and deer. Ticks only hang onto a body for a short while and drink only a tiny amount of blood. But some can spread deadly diseases.

Ticks have smaller relatives called mites that may also live on your body. Most mites don't drink blood, though. Some drink oils at the base of hairs. Others feed on dead skin. Mites are all around you all of the time—on the plants in your backyard, in the soil beneath your feet, even in your bed as you doze.

Read on to learn more about ticks and mites—a fascinating, diverse, but rarely seen group of animals.

Ticks are tiny creatures with eight legs. This one is a called a deer tick. That is because at some time in its life it will climb onto a deer to suck its blood.

What Are Ticks?

Opposite page:
Spiders are close relatives of ticks. They both belong to a group called arachnids. Arachnids may look a little like insects, but they all have eight legs, not six, as insects do.

Ticks are arachnids, tiny relatives of animals like spiders and scorpions. Ticks are part of a larger group of similar creatures called mites. Mites come in a wide variety. They live practically everywhere. They also feed on an incredible range of different foods. They eat anything from rotting leaves to dead skin, plant cells, and even worms and other mites.

Ticks feed only on blood and only the blood of certain groups of vertebrates (backboned animals) at that. Ticks are divided into two groups. Soft ticks have soft, stretchy skins and feed only briefly on their victims, or hosts, before dropping off unnoticed. The other group, the hard ticks, feed for many days at a time. Their skins are tough to resist grooming by the irritated host. Because they are more limited in their choice of foods, there are fewer types of ticks than mites—around 860 species. Biologists have no real idea of the number of types of mites. There are at least 45,000, but there may be many, many more.

Where Do Ticks Live?

Mites form one of the most widespread of all animal groups. They are found in every habitat on Earth, from the deep oceans to ponds and streams, and from high mountains to scorching deserts. They are also one of the few creatures able to live on mainland Antarctica.

Ticks, however, can only live wherever their hosts occur. Tick hosts include mammals, birds, and reptiles. One species of tick even lives on a type of toad. Ticks are especially common on animals that live on grasslands, such as cattle, buffalo, and antelope. Tall grass provides the ticks with a suitable jumping off point. As large grazing animals brush their way through the grass, the ticks can easily hitch a ride.

Some ticks feed on penguins, so there are ticks living even in the icy wastes of Antarctica. These ticks are living on the dung of chin-strap penguins. They will soon climb onto the penguins and suck their blood.

Ancient Animals

Ticks and mites have been around for a very long time. There are preserved remains of mites 380 million years old. Mites may have lived differently long ago. Scientists have found 350 million-year-old remains of wood with tiny tunnels in them. These tunnels contain preserved droppings of mites. So we know that long ago, mites bored in wood.

Ticks appeared much more recently than mites. The earliest tick discovered so far dates from 90 million years ago. It was found preserved in a piece of orange stone called amber. Amber was once the sap of trees, and the tick got stuck in it before it hardened. This ancient tick parasite may once have fed on the blood of dinosaurs!

We know that ticks and other arachnids lived long ago because they were preserved in amber, like the spider at the bottom here.

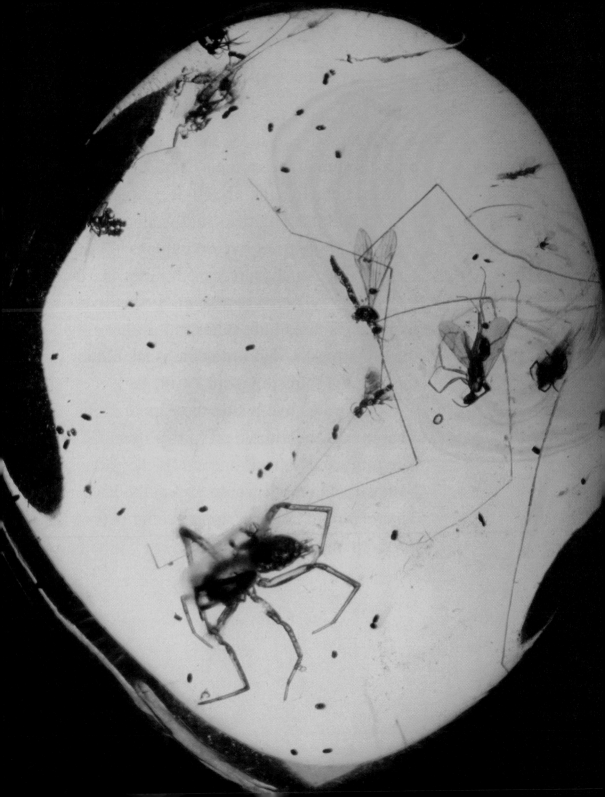

Strange Places to Live

Ticks and many mites are parasites. That means they live in or on the bodies of other animals some time in their lives. Black-legged, or deer, ticks live mainly on deer. Rabbit ticks live on rabbits. Dog ticks and wood ticks live on dogs. Some ticks live on humans.

Many dogs may suffer from mites that live in their ears. There are also mites that live inside bees' breathing tubes, mites that cling to crayfish gills, and mites that suck blood through the joints on a spider's legs.

Some mites live inside the ears of moths. That makes the moth deaf in the affected ear. The mites only attack one ear. If they attacked both ears, the moth would go totally deaf. Then it would not hear approaching bats. So moth and mites might be eaten by the bat.

Foul Foods

Just like ticks, many mites are parasites of people. Some of these mites eat truly disgusting foods. Follicle mites live inside follicles—the roots of hairs—on people's bodies. There they feed by sipping tiny drops of oil released by the follicles to keep the skin supple and in good condition.

Your skin is constantly rubbed off and replaced with new skin. The old skin provides food for dust mites. Dust mites often live in mattresses and pillows where there is plenty of old skin.

Scabies mites prefer to live on a person's body. They dig little tunnels through the skin as they feed on fluids from just beneath the surface. That makes their unfortunate victim's skin very, very itchy.

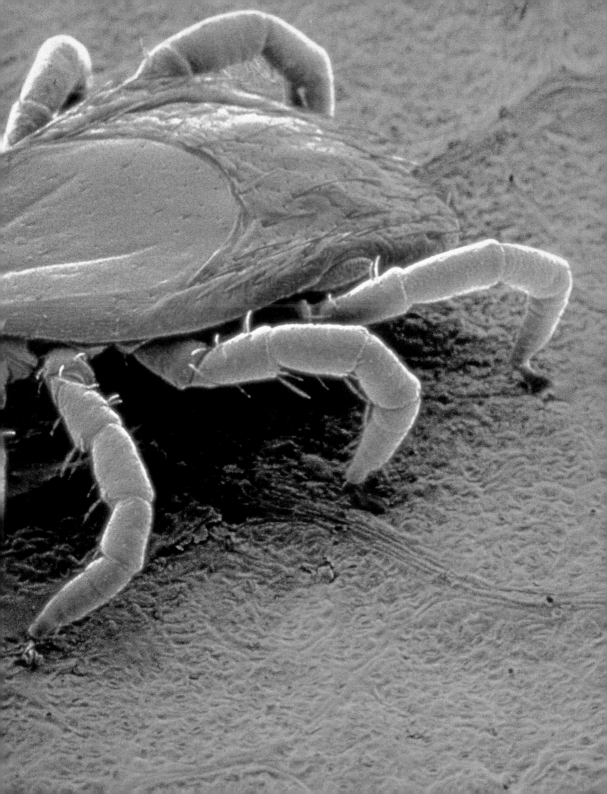

A tick's mouthparts need to be sharp to pierce its victim's skin. In the center is the hypostome.

The Quest for Food

Unlike mites, ticks eat just one thing—the blood of animals like birds and mammals. When hard ticks detect the breath of a possible host or its body heat, they quickly clamber up a grass stalk. There they hold their front legs out straight. Biologists call this behavior questing. If the host brushes past the tick, it quickly climbs on.

A tick feeds by piercing its hosts's skin with a sharp mouthpart called the hypostome. Hooks on the hypostome anchor the tick. The tick dribbles saliva around its mouth. This hardens like glue to stick the tick in place. Tick saliva also keeps the host's blood from flowing freely and forming a scab. And it helps prevent the host's body defenses from driving away the tick.

When it is done feeding, the tick dissolves the glue and tumbles to the ground. A hard tick may increase its body weight by 600 times after just one meal.

Detecting Victims

When questing for victims, ticks rely a great deal on smell. They have an important sensory pit on their head, called Haller's organ. It detects chemicals in the air.

Some of these chemicals are called pheromones. They are released by ticks as they feed. When other ticks sense these pheromones, it sends them into a frenzy as they try to join in the feast. Other chemicals are important for finding food too. Host animals have a chemical called squalene on their skins that ticks are attracted to. Ticks are also drawn to carbon dioxide, a waste gas breathed out by animals. Other gases in breath serve to attract ticks too.

Ticks also use other cues besides smell to help them find hosts. They include vibrations in the air or through the ground made by walking feet!

Two creatures are after this deer's blood—the mosquitoes in the air and the ticks infecting its ear.

19

Softly, Softly

Hard ticks feed between one and three times in their lives, with each meal lasting for several weeks. Soft ticks feed in a different way. Rather than questing for food, most soft ticks stay in the nests of their hosts instead. That allows them the chance to feed many times in their lives. The ticks wait for the host to return to its nest before climbing on to feed for a short time. They increase their weight around ten times before dropping off. The females then lay eggs and wait for the host to return so they can repeat the process.

Soft ticks do not search for hosts as hard ticks do. If their host fails to return, they have to wait until another animal occupies the nest before feeding again. To cope with this uncertainty, soft ticks are amazingly resistant to starvation. They can survive for up to six years between meals!

Opposite page:
Little birds called oxpeckers are friends to many African animals like this giraffe. Oxpeckers feed on the ticks that suck on the animals' blood.

Deadly Disease Carriers

Opposite page: *This dog tick is the carrier of the terrible disease Rocky Mountain spotted fever. When it bites a dog, the dog may become infected with the disease.*

Many ticks carry in their bodies germs that cause terrible diseases. When these ticks bite a person, they can inject the germs into the victim's body. The germs then make the victim ill. Lyme disease, for example, is caused by the bite of a black-legged tick carrying a certain kind of bacteria. People with Lyme disease suffer from painful joints and fevers. Another disease carried by ticks, Rocky Mountain spotted fever, is even worse and can kill. This illness is transmitted by dog ticks, and it causes damage to the kidneys and lungs.

It is not just people that are vulnerable to diseases carried by ticks and mites. Varroa mites, for example, attack honeybees. Many colonies of honeybees have died off over recent years, since the mites pass on a disease organism as they feed that kills the bees.

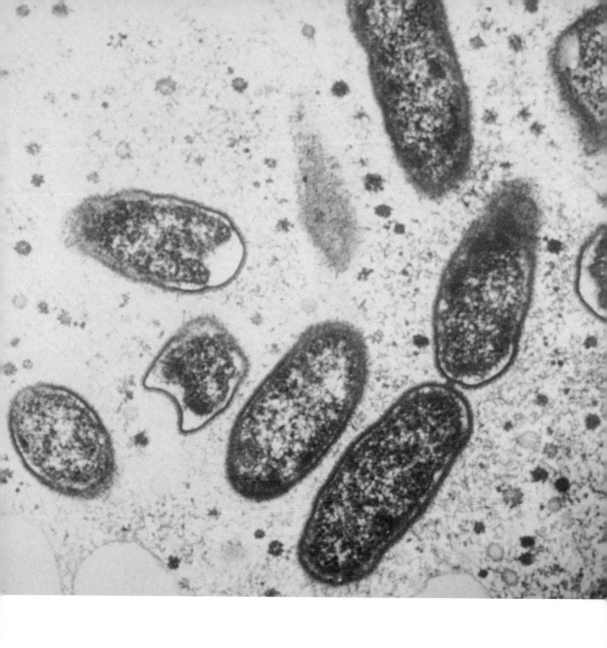

Rocky Mountain spotted fever is caused by these Rickettsia bacteria, which are carried by ticks.

Other Tick-borne Diseases

Animals that carry disease organisms from place to place are called vectors. Mosquitoes are the most devastating vectors. Diseases carried by mosquitoes kill millions of people every year. But ticks run them a close second.

Ticks transmit a huge variety of disease-causing organisms. As well as Lyme disease and Rocky Mountain spotted fever, ticks can spread a disease called babesiosis. Babesia parasites invade and destroy red blood cells. Babesiosis can kill cattle within a few weeks. It attacks rodents and dogs, too. Every year ten or so people are also infected with babesiosis in the United States.

Ticks also spread the deadly disease tick-borne typhus. A week after a bite from a typhus-carrying tick a victim suffers a raging fever and throbbing headaches. A rash spreads from the site of the tick bite. Tick-borne typhus is very dangerous for old people or those already weak with other illnesses. One in 15 people infected with this disease die.

Awful Allergies

It is not just disease organisms that cause illness after a tick bite. Some people have severe allergic reactions to tick saliva. The allergic reaction is caused by the victim's internal defense system going into overdrive in response to the presence of the tick saliva.

Sometimes the allergic response can paralyze parts of the victim's body. That is especially likely if the tick bites at the base of the skull or on the back of the head. This is called tick toxicosis or tick paralysis. While terrifying, the paralysis wears off after the offending tick is removed, and the victim soon recovers. Fortunately, tick toxicosis is very rare in North America.

The girl on the right had an allergic reaction to tick saliva. Her mom is giving her medication to cure it.

Finding a Partner

Ticks are slow moving and cannot fly far and wide to look for mates. Simply wandering around through the forest or grassland is not a good way to find others. So most ticks wait until they are safely settled on the body of a suitable host before beginning their search for a good partner.

Male ticks are smaller than the females. When they find a female, they mate with her quickly. Sometimes they may even mate while the female is busy feeding on the host's blood. The male dies soon after mating is completed, but the female drops from the host to the ground to lay her eggs.

A female black-legged tick has one last meal of blood from its deer host before mating. It will then drop off the deer to lay its eggs.

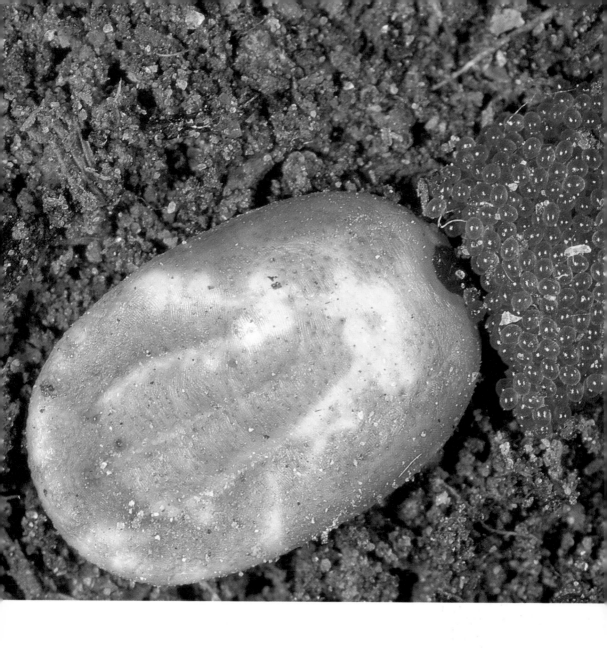

After mating, sheep ticks drop off their sheep host and lay 24-48 eggs on the ground.

Growing Up

As ticks grow up, their lives go through three stages. When it first hatches from its egg, a tick is a grub or larva with just six legs, like an insect. After a short time the young tick grows two more legs and enters the second stage of its life, called a nymph. The third and final stage of the tick's life is as an adult. That is when it mates or lays its eggs and dies.

It may take a hard tick three years to go through its life stages in cold places, but much less in the tropics. It has just one meal of blood in each life stage. A soft tick has many more but can survive years without a meal.

A tick does not grow steadily like you but in a series of spurts. Before each spurt it sheds its skin. That is called molting. Then before the new skin hardens, it swells by feeding on blood. A hard tick molts twice before it becomes an adult—once to change from larva to nymph and once to change from nymph to adult. Soft ticks molt up to seven times as nymphs, growing a little each time.

Different Lives

Hard ticks need to time their lives to ensure they find a host at the right time. So different hard ticks have different life cycles. Some hard ticks, called one-host ticks, feed on only one host, such as a cow, for all three of their life stages. A one-host tick sucks the blood of the cow as a larva and changes into a nymph. It then sucks the cow's blood again before changing into an adult. Adults then suck the cow's blood one last time. The males then mate and die, and the females drop off the host to lay their eggs.

A two-host tick feeds off two different hosts. It sucks its first host's blood once as a larva and once as a nymph. When it becomes an adult, it drops off to find a new host for its final blood meal. Males then mate and die, and females drop off to lay eggs. Three-host ticks feed off three different hosts, one at each stage of their lives. A three-host tick may start life as a larva on a squirrel, live on a rabbit as a nymph, and spend its adult life on a cow.

This oxpecker bird is looking for the adult ticks that are feeding on this buffalo.

Enemies of Ticks and Mites

Mites have many natural enemies to contend with. They are attacked by a whole range of tiny foes, including thrips, ladybugs, and even other mites. Ticks are larger than mites and so they represent a decent snack for some larger creatures.

Ticks are particularly vulnerable after feeding, when they are bloated with blood. Fire ants, mongooses, and mice all feast on well-fed ticks. They are also a favorite food of birds such as oxpeckers and egrets. These birds remove parasites from large mammals like elephants and buffalo. The mammals benefit by having the pesky ticks removed, while the birds get an easy, nutritious meal.

In Africa and Asia one of the tick's biggest enemies is the mongoose. A mongoose is a small predator about the size of a cat.

After-dark Antics

Opposite page:
Blood is the only liquid this sheep tick ever drinks in its life. It must keep its water needs to a minimum by moving only at night.

Most ticks do most of their moving after night has fallen. That is because, like other animals such as insects, ticks breathe through holes in their bodies called spiracles. Insects lose water through their spiracles. Most insects can easily top up their water supplies by drinking or feeding on water-rich food.

Ticks cannot do that since they feed only rarely. So they must conserve as much water as possible by moving around only at night, when it is cooler and less water is lost.

Most ticks do not have eyes. They know when it is dark, though, from the two sets of light receptors that run in rows along the sides of their heads.

Water Problems

As we have seen, getting water can be tricky for a tick. Waiting on a grass stalk for a suitable host can soon dry out the little animal, especially in windy or hot weather.

You might think that a tick could simply drink from pools of water trapped in the undergrowth. However, ticks cannot afford to do that. They actually avoid pools of water. That is because such water may contain germs that would kill the tick. Instead, ticks head toward a damp plant and let water evaporating from the plant collect on their mouthparts. They then suck the water in through their mouths.

Ticks don't drink from pools.
Instead, they head for damp plants.
There, they wait for water to collect
like dew drops on their mouthparts,
ready for them to suck up.

Small Creatures

Opposite page:
Velvet mites are among the biggest mites. But they are still no bigger than your fingernail. They live in the soil most of the year. They only emerge for a few hours after rain to feed on their prey.

Ticks are very small. Most are less than 0.2 inches (4 millimeters) long. Ticks are slightly bigger just after they eat. The largest ticks can measure up to 1.2 inches (3 centimeters) long after a good meal.

Mites are even smaller than ticks, and most can only be seen through a microscope. The smallest measure just 0.01 inches (0.2 millimeters) long—five would fit onto the period at the end of this sentence. The biggest are velvet mites—but even they are only 0.4 inches (8 millimeters) long. Velvet mites have bright red or orange bodies and are very hairy. The adults live on and eat the bodies of insects, especially termites, that they catch in the soil. The young of many species specialize in living on grasshoppers and locusts.

Avoiding Tick Bites

Getting bitten by a tick can be a serious matter. Whenever you visit the great outdoors, it pays to take some antitick precautions. Try to avoid tick-infested areas, especially from April through September—that is the period of peak tick activity. Wear boots or other tough footwear and long pants that cover your legs tucked into your socks. Shorts and sandals may be more comfortable during the hot summer months, but they provide no sort of barrier to a hungry tick!

Also, keep your arms covered to leave as little skin exposed as possible. When you get back from your walk, remove your clothes, and carefully check your body for ticks either wandering around or already feeding. The earlier a tick is found and removed, the less chance a person stands of being infected by a tick-borne parasite.

Opposite page:
This is a cattle tick. But it can easily attack you if you're out in the country near cows in the summer.

Further Tips for Foiling Ticks

Ticks are extremely resistant to most chemicals used to control pests. However, there are a few chemicals that are designed to target ticks. If you are going into a tick-infested area, it is worth applying tick repellent to your skin and clothing. It is important to spray your socks and the legs of your pants too, since ticks can easily get in there.

Pets such as dogs can be hosts for ticks, so they must be treated with pesticides from time to time. Try to keep weeds and grasses cut short in your backyard too. That will reduce the chances of ticks climbing up onto your body from tall stems.

Words to Know

Allergy A nasty reaction of the body to a substance to which it has become very sensitive.

Amber Hardened ancient tree sap.

Grub see Larva.

Host An animal or plant on which a parasite lives.

Hypostome The sharp mouthpart of a tick. It has hooks on the end for catching onto the skin of a tick's victim

Larva The first stage in the life of small creatures such as ticks.

Molt For a mite or tick, molting means shedding its outer casing in order to grow.

Nymph The young of ticks, mites, and insects such as dragonflies and termites.

Parasite An organism that feeds on or in another organism without usually killing it.

Pesticide A substance for destroying ticks and other pests.

Pheromone A chemical released by a tick or other creature that affects the behavior of other creatures of its kind.

Predator An animal that eats other animals.

Prey Animals that become food for predators.

Questing The behavior seen when a tick searches for a host.

Spiracle Breathing holes in the side of a tick's body.

INDEX

Cover Photo: Still Pictures: Volker Steger
Photo Credits: Bruce Coleman: Jane Burton 7, Kim Taylor 39; **Corbis:** AFP 27, Lester V. Bergman 24, Clouds Hill Imaging Ltd. 31, Roger De La Harpe 28, Raymond Gehman 19, Darrell Gulin 40, Peter Johnson 35, Wolfgang Kaehler 20, Layne Kennedy 11, George D. Lepp 44, Carl & Ann Purcell 36; **NHPA:** Nigel J. Dennis 43; **Oxford Scientific Films:** Paulo De Oliveira 32, Rick Price/SAL 8; **Science Photo Library:** Eye of Science 16; **Still Pictures:** Volker Steger 14/15; **USDA/Agricultural Research Service:** Scott Bauer 4, 23.